HOW TO INCREASE YOUR BRAIN-POWER AND INTELLIGENCE
with tips on excelling in IQ & aptitude tests

KERWIN MATHEW

HOW TO INCREASE YOUR BRAIN-POWER AND
INTELLIGENCE
with tips on excelling in IQ & aptitude tests

PREFACE

The brain can in some way be compared to a car engine. The car may have a powerful engine but the driver plays an important role too. Granted, that a powerful car engine makes all the difference. But the driver must know how to take care of and handle the car and car engine to make the car perform smoothly and efficiently. The same goes for the owner of the brain. The brain is even better and more powerful than a car engine. Like a muscle, it can grow better and stronger with exercise, which has been confirmed.

This book is about making the brain better, stronger and more efficient. The author has been experimenting with certain forms of brain training which have proven helpful and would like to share all this in this book.

Kerwin Mathew, Ph.D., PE, CMfgT, CPM

CONTENTS

1 INTRODUCTION

Francis Galton, a nineteenth-century British scientist, originated the earliest organized thought on the concept of intelligence testing. He came up with the idea of investigating the relationship between heredity and human ability after Charles Darwin published *The Origin of Species* in 1859. The prevailing thought of the time was that the human race had only a handful of really intelligent people and a small number of mentally deficient people, while the greater part of the population fell within a narrow band of intelligence. Galton believed that mental traits were based on physical factors and were inherited, just like blood type and eye color. His work was also influenced by Quetelet, a Belgian statistician, who was the first to apply statistical methods to the study of human characteristics. It was Quetelet who first postulated the concept of a normal distribution of intelligence on a bell curve. Galton published his ideas in a book titled *Hereditary Genius*, which is considered the first scientific investigation on the concept of intelligence.

However, it was the French psychologist Alfred Binet who first devised a test to assess human intelligence. Binet had been interested in developing a test to measure intelligence in children. He commenced trial testing with Parisian students to determine what the normal abilities would be for a certain age and identify those who were below the norm. In 1904, the French government commissioned Binet to find a method of differentiating between children who were intellectually normal and those who were inferior, with the object of putting the inferior children into special schools where they would receive additional schooling. Binet's test was called the Binet Scale; it was at this time that the phrase "intelligence quotient", or, "IQ" first made its appearance.

An American school administrator, H. H. Goddard, who

found out about Binet's work in France, decided to use the latter's test to screen students for his school. After knowledge of Goddard's use of Binet's test spread across the country, a Stanford professor, Lewis Terman, worked on revising Binet's test; in 1916, he published his seminal work, the *Stanford Revision of the Binet-Simon Scale of Intelligence* (also known as the Stanford-Binet), which quickly became the gold standard for intelligence testing in the United States for the next several decades.

When the U.S. entered World War I, its army was faced with the problem of sorting huge numbers of draftees into various army positions. To overcome this problem, the army assembled an ad hoc committee of the top psychologists in the country to design an intelligence test for new recruits. Lewis Terman was on this committee. The committee adopted a standard test for all new recruits, which, by 1919, was taken by nearly two million soldiers. The army's test put intelligence testing on the map and its popularity exploded since then.

Many companies, building on the army's popular intelligence test, began their own forms of intelligence testing to determine potential new employees, who to promote, and so on. The tests also quickly became widely used in education. In fact, by the 1950s nearly every school district in the U.S. was conducting some form of intelligence testing.

By the 1960s there were doubts raised about the cultural biases inherent in intelligence tests. The New York City Board of Education then eliminated all IQ testing in their school system. This was followed by many other school districts, who blamed racial and culturally loaded questions for large gaps in scores amongst certain groups and ethnicities.

By the 1980s ideas on intelligence testing were changing,

with Howard Gardner introducing the concept of multiple intelligences. Gardner defined seven distinct intelligences, viz., linguistic, logical-mathematical, spatial, bodily-kinesthetic, musical, interpersonal and intrapersonal intelligences. His work on multiple intelligences quickly spread through the industry, with many tests remodeled to reflect the new views on intelligence. Gardner's ideas resulted in the modern intelligence test. Intelligence tests began to find their way back into the educational system in many forms, from IQ tests to standardized tests such as the SAT.

Today, the intelligence test has been refined to an extent never thought possible in the past. The IQ test is now considered by many to be not only the most important achievement in the field of psychology, but one of the crowning achievements of modern society. The IQ test has been listed as one of the 20 most significant scientific discoveries of the century along with the transistor, flight, DNA and nuclear fission by the American Academy for the Advancement of Science in 1989. As IQ tests are apparently here to stay, it pays for us to understand them thoroughly and learn how to do well in them.

2 CULTIVATE THE USEFUL KINDS OF INTELLIGENCE

We all evidently know what intelligence is and know it at once when an intelligent person shows and acts it. Generally, it is regarded as the power of comprehension or understanding as well as the ability to tackle problems well. We are all the time judging the intelligence of people we encounter, whether consciously or subconsciously, whether we are really aware of it or not. We may regard someone a genius just because he understands and masters a subject easily and well while we may face immense difficulty with the mastery of the same subject. The fact is that our intelligence may be below average while that of the "genius" may just be average or slightly above average. The point here is that the judgment of intelligence is subjective.

What then actually is intelligence, to put it on a firmer footing? The following are some possible definitions:-

[1] Ability to solve problems well
[2] Ability to think logically
[3] Ability to think clearly
[4] Ability to draw on a large store of information
[5] Ability to set and achieve goals
[6] Ability to utilize a good vocabulary
[7] Ability to analyze and use information
[8] Ability to achieve practical results besides having a good
    theoretical understanding of the subject

We will take a look at Howard Gardner's concept of multiple intelligences, which have now gained importance. We should cultivate as much of these intelligences as possible, the more intelligences we are endowed with the more intelligent we actually are.

MULTIPLE INTELLIGENCES (MI)

Howard Gardner revolutionized the field of intelligence theory with the publication of *Frames of Mind* in 1983, replacing traditional measures of intelligence with an intuitive approach. Gardner's theories have been most robust in American education. He posits eight distinct intelligences, distinguishing them from mere "talents" or "abilities". Entire schools have been set up based on his theories. In the workplace where it is less applicable so far, MI theory is solidly grounded in its applications to the person's job search and success within his chosen field.

Multiple intelligences are about how smart a person acts and not how smart a person is or can be. This is a reversal of the past theoretical underpinning of intelligence. MI theory is about the interaction between eight distinct yet interrelated categories. Each person is intelligent in the real world with some regularity depending on context and environment. For example, in the workplace, a person may interact with colleagues, propose new ideas to his supervisor, solve problems between himself and colleagues who may not think alike. Though scoring highly within a particular intelligence may guide his choice of activity or vocation, he has to go beyond simple self-labeling such as labeling himself "linguistically intelligent". It is likely that more than one intelligence is utilized in most careers though the intelligences are distinct. The intelligent person may actively develop many intelligences at once regardless of vocation or context in order to avoid being typecast into categories.

According to MI theory, each intelligence is based on neuroimaging techniques which isolate distinct brain activity while engaged in specific activities. One's environment, ranging from one's workplace to the country in which one lives, may have a great impact on the intelligences developed within each respective milieu. Much research which contributed to MI theory has resulted from studies of persons with localized brain damage that negated the victim's ability to perform complete tasks within a specific intelligence.

Based on studies which isolate different parts of the brain engaged with diverse activities, people are found to be biologically wired to excel in one or more areas. The ability of a person to utilize these intelligences and apply them is preceded by the need to "know oneself", which is required for the development of intrapersonal intelligence. As an evolving theory, several ideas have been considered for possible inclusion in the overall definition such as digital intelligence, spiritual intelligence and sexual intelligence. Let us examine Gardner's eight intelligences, which are presented below:-

[1] Linguistic Intelligence

Linguistic intelligence involves the use of language to facilitate understanding through the spoken or written word. Intelligent persons endowed with linguistic intelligence typically have an easier time mastering the demands of a scholastic environment and thrive in settings in which they can achieve success writing papers and proposals, or authoring employment manuals, e.g., human resources manuals. On the other hand, the person with a high level of linguistic intelligence may find himself or herself ostracized for appearing arrogant or snobbish, using "big" words which normally do not enter into everyday discourse. Once understood and embraced, the linguistically intelligent person may find an environment in which his or her talents can blossom and, ultimately, improve the working conditions for himself and his peers.

The linguistically intelligent person is well-versed with the subtleties of language, which is an asset for those in professions requiring this ability, e.g., lawyers, who review briefs and twist words to benefit from an argument. Doctors also need high levels of linguistic intelligence in order to absorb voluminous amounts of information and integrate them into practice with patients. Well written emails by those with high linguistic intelligence would be a communication boon.

The linguistically intelligent person, commonly misperceived as being "talkative", is able to convey richness of ideas with a minimum of words, a large vocabulary being typically his hallmark. He may spend leisure time working on crossword puzzles, anagrams and other similarly challenging puzzles, he may maintain a detailed journal, or he may write an online blog or interact with others on a public forum board.

[2] Musical Intelligence
Musical intelligence, which may manifest itself in the form of production, discrimination, composition, or aural entertainment, encompasses the ability to derive great intellectual enjoyment from sound. The musically intelligent person is capable of appreciating the subtleties in sound, timbre, harmony and pitch, i.e., capable of enjoying music. Music in the background may affect the musically intelligent person, even when he is at work.

The musically intelligent person will naturally pursue the musical arts with great vigor away from the workplace. Musically intelligent people may even create their own musical compositions.

[3] Logical-Mathematical Intelligence
The person endowed with logical-mathematical intelligence possesses the ability to see abstract images and work towards goals in a sensible manner. These skills, like linguistic intelligence, yield high levels of success for those engaged in academic pursuits. In the

workplace, those who have these skills are highly valued. The ability to formulate a coherent argument and present it to others is valued in almost any activity, e.g., in the legal and architectural fields, and, this necessitates high levels of linguistic intelligence as well.

Logical-mathematical intelligence, which is the ability to conceptualize theories and enumerate steps to test them, is highly prized in scientific pursuits.

[4] Spatial Intelligence
A person with a high level of spatial intelligence will transform visual images into concrete objects for others to see. A person endowed with this intelligence may not get lost in an unfamiliar place and may easily navigate there. Such a person will be capable of synthesizing multiple ideas into a unifying principle that crystallizes seemingly distinct concepts. Gender differences within this intelligence are apparently pronounced, with males achieving higher levels than females; to eliminate this gender gap, researchers are training females to score equally on measures of mental rotation. Engineers and architects, e.g., are strong in spatial intelligence. This intelligence may be highly prized and unique in vocations where diverse people need unifying constructs. The ability to visualize does not require a person to physically see; this implies that people suffering from blindness can have high levels of spatial intelligence. Those strong in this area may refer to themselves as "right-brained", as the right half of the brain is responsible for spatial intelligence.

[5] Interpersonal Intelligence
Those with high levels of interpersonal intelligence display high levels of leadership, influence and extroversion. Interpersonally intelligent people tend to be charismatic, likeable and sought out socially by others,

being natural masters of group dynamics. In the workplace, they often counsel and persuade others, and explain difficult concepts with ease. Interpersonally intelligent people are likely to thrive in careers in which success is based on good sales techniques. Those endowed with interpersonal intelligence are capable of sensing the needs and desires of others and are suited for the helping professions, e.g., psychologist, social worker and clergy.

Interpersonally intelligent people tend to derive pleasure from frequent contact with others and may spend their leisure hours with a wide variety of people outside the workplace.

[6] Intrapersonal Intelligence
The intrapersonally intelligent person has a keen awareness of others' feelings, goals and motivations, and may be best suited for professions requiring work with others. People endowed with this intelligence, who also have sympathy for those who are less fortunate, are ideally suited for charitable work as a vocation or hobby. This kind of intelligence will also serve those in other professions well, e.g., engineers and accountants who have to deal with other people.

[7] Bodily-Kinesthetic Intelligence
Bodily-kinesthetic intelligence is the ability to utilize parts of the body to solve problems or create tangible products. It is about physical dexterity such as sporting prowess, fast and accurate typing skill, the surgeon's nimble touch, the dancer's graceful movements, the martial artist's steps and the actor's rendition of a famous person's gestures. Those endowed with this intelligence are capable of executing fine physical acts with ease.

[8] Naturalist Intelligence

Naturalist intelligence has recently been included in the growing list of intelligences. The person with a high level of natural intelligence will be much capable of identifying patterns, classifying and cataloging, and he is likely to be one who enjoys outdoor activities. This is in fact an organizational skill which is highly valued in corporations. This is the ability to create order out of chaos, e.g., determining differences between birds while bird-watching and categorizing book collections for sale.

There are evidently much more than the above eight intelligences. The human intellect is complex and seems to have infinite capacity. It is claimed that humans only utilize about ten per cent of their full mental capacity. It is really up to us to train and more fully utilize our mental faculties.

3 TIPS ON EXCELLING IN IQ AND APTITUDE TESTS

Many of us are concerned about our ability to do well in tests of mental capacity and aptitude. This is understandable as society today is a "test" or "examination" society wherein practically everyone is being judged all the time, in their workplace, in school, in college, in the army, in the social setting, and even in the home. Of course intelligence and aptitude tests are not absolute or fool-proof tests of mental ability. But at least, they are more reliable, and more objective, than mere observation of a person's character and/or appearance, in judging his mental capacity. Many colleges in the U.S. and other parts of the world require sufficiently high scores in the SAT, GRE, GMAT or other aptitude tests for admission. The army, e.g., also subject their recruits to intelligence tests to determine their army vocations. The civil service has also conducted tests for their recruits, e.g., the British civil service. In China in the past mandarins or civil servants had to pass stringent examinations, with the imperial examinations which were the highest level examinations that were equivalent to a Ph.D. examination being the standard entry requirement for top flight mandarins. Many companies also subject their job applicants to aptitude tests. Those who want to gain admission to the high IQ societies such as the popular Mensa also need to do sufficiently well in the respective societies' intelligence tests, whose formats may differ from each other. Many, e.g., had to repeat the Mensa IQ tests a number of times before they attained the score that qualified them for membership of Mensa. With test practices it is possible to increase one's IQ by a whopping 15 to 20 points. The author himself had sat for quite a number of intelligence and aptitude tests for some of the reasons stated above and had also done intelligence tests for the challenge and fun. At one time he had even thought of trying for Mensa membership but had stopped short of doing so thinking that it would be too "vain" or "show off" to be a Mensa member. Instead he took other "tests", e.g., solving famous long unsolved problems, which are even more challenging.

Actually, the questions asked in IQ and aptitude tests are not really that difficult, compared to, e.g., the level of the long unsolved problems in science and mathematics. Anyone with *sufficient patience, motivation, persistence and practice*, should have no problem answering all or most of them correctly. The reader may here wonder how such tests differentiate between the genius or extremely intelligent, the merely highly intelligent, the average in intelligence and the below average in intelligence if they are not really that difficult and could be correctly answered by the highly motivated and persistent. The determinant here for excelling in the IQ and aptitude tests is evidently speed in answering the questions, i.e., speed of thought, which implies that the faster a person thinks the more intelligent he is. In fact, practically all IQ and aptitude tests would not allot sufficient time for completing the tests, expecting the test-taker to rush through the tests. Therefore, speed in doing the tests is important. This question of speed is actually a simplistic view of intelligence held by those who produce the IQ and aptitude tests. Of course easy questions could be answered relatively speedily. This would not work for the very difficult questions such as those of the long unsolved problems in science and mathematics, which require long and deep thinking, some of which have been unsolved for hundreds, even thousands, of years. In fact, fast thinking tends not to be deep or reflective thinking; deep, reflective thinking which requires the thinker to mentally explore further would definitely take up more time, possibly very much more time. Like the case of the fast, short distance runner and the slow, long distance runner in sports, there are the fast, short-time thinker and the slow, methodical, careful, long-time thinker whose motto may be "slow and steady wins the race". The mathematical genius and Nobel laureate John Nash of *A Beautiful Mind* fame belongs to the latter category of thinkers - while others would give up on a tough problem a long time ago he would persist and try for years to crack the problem. A similar kind of thinker was the scientific genius Einstein, who took around ten years to formulate his Special Theory of Relativity and General Theory of Relativity, and had spent many fruitless years working on the Unified Field Theory till death and without any success. Since the producers of IQ and aptitude tests try to be smart by "outsmarting" us, their test-takers, their "guinea pigs", we should try to be smart and "outsmart" them, i.e., beat them at their own game. The reader may also wonder whether it is necessary for the test producers to be more intelligent than the test-takers and if they are not more intelligent than the test-takers what right do they have to test the test-takers. Well, at least they are smart enough to convince the testing authority that they are smart enough for the job.

Without further ado, we shall find some way to beat these test-producing smarties at their own game. The reader should pay attention to the following and execute them:-

Tips On Excelling In IQ And Aptitude Tests
[1]   Choose or target your IQ or aptitude test, e.g., Mensa IQ test or SAT, which best suits your capability, if possible.
[2]   Obtain past test papers of your selected test where possible, study them and carefully note their format. Deconstruct the tests. Get used to the questions asked and the methodologies involved.
[3]   Practice doing as many of such IQ or aptitude tests as possible, subjecting yourself to the actual test conditions. It is very important for you to get used to working fast without making mistakes under pressure. (Compare: The athlete training really hard to break the record for the 100-meter dash.) Plan/think

of/visualize your strategies for the actual test.

[4] Though it is important to try your best and put in your best effort for the test, *do not make it a "life and death" thing as this could cause unnecessary nervousness and anxiety which would affect your test performance.*

[5] *Treat the test as an interesting challenge and enjoy taking the challenge.* Aim for *optimum performance.* Don't overdo it and over-stress yourself.

[6] Have a good night's rest before the actual test. Feel fresh and confident. (Before the test you may wash your face to make yourself feel fresh.) It is very important to be calm. Practice Zen calmness. Be in a good, optimistic mood. *Warm up the brain by doing a few IQ/aptitude test questions just before the test.* Be really in the mood to face the challenge of the test. That is, *make sure you are mentally prepared and confident for the test.* (On the other hand, if the test-taker were depressed and fearful, his test performance would be adversely affected.) Doing plenty of test practices and doing well in them would bring confidence, optimism and good mood to the test-taker when taking the actual test. That is, good test preparation is important. As time is the essence in the test, there is little time to think or figure out the method for arriving at the correct answer. *Important: The test-taker should be so familiar with such tests (through really good test preparation with practice tests), that he instinctively knows the method of arriving at the correct answer with hardly any hard thinking and figuring, thus saving plenty of time and making it possible to complete all the questions on time and obtaining a perfect score.*

[7] Have a good meal (especially of food deemed to boost mental energy or mental capacity if this will bring more confidence to do well in the test) before the test, but, do not have too heavy a meal as a heavy meal tends to make you drowsy and blunt your mental capacity.

[8] It is of course very important to be *alert* and to *avoid*

carelessness during the test.

[9] During the test, read all instructions and questions very carefully. Underline or highlight the keywords of instructions and questions. Make sure you really understand the instructions and questions, pay close attention to the keywords which are to act as reminders for you to answer to the point, and answer *strictly to the point* and not out of point.

[10] The test will be likely to offer barely enough time to complete, as its goal is to gage speed and efficiency of thought. Therefore, good time-keeping is really important. Plan and allocate your timing for each question. Be persistent and determined to answer the questions correctly and within the allocated time limits but do not spend too much time on any question. If stumped, do not panic, do not hang on too long, guess (if there is no penalty for wrong answers) and move on quickly once the allocated time is up; otherwise it will not be possible to complete all the questions on time resulting in loss of precious marks especially when there is no time to answer the easy questions whose answers you know.

[11] During the actual test, it is even more important to have the above-said Zen calmness. Some test questions are expected to be difficult. Do not panic. You must maintain the said Zen calmness. When one panics, one cannot think clearly and straight. However, with Zen calmness, clarity and speed of thought are possible. Utilize calming techniques, e.g., deep breathing, et al. *Remember: It is very important to be calm and not to panic in order to be able to think straight, think clearly, so that even the toughest question can be successfully tackled.*

[12] It is important to pace yourself. *You should work as fast as possible but not so fast that you make careless mistakes.* (While practicing the tests earlier on, you

should have cultivated the speed of working you are comfortable with, i.e., cultivate a great enough speed without making careless mistakes.)

[13] Be calm and confident throughout the test. (This would come from thorough test practices and high scores achieved in the practice tests under actual test conditions; you would then be sure and confident of your capability. Remember that all Olympic champions and other very high achievers train and practice very hard. There is no short-cut and lazy way to high achievements. Remember the 10,000-hour-practice rule which implies the great importance of hard work and consistent practice.)

[14] A good general rule will be to answer all the easier questions first and tackle the more difficult questions after that.

[15] If you can't answer the tough question, make a guess (especially if wrong answers would not be penalized), put a mark against the question, and return to consider the answer again later when you have time.

[16] For objective questions with given answers to choose from, first eliminate all the clearly wrong answers, then select the right answer from the rest.

[17] For [16] above make sure you tick/write the answer in the correct box.

[18] It is important to write legibly and neatly for marks would be lost if the marker could not decipher your handwriting and did not award the marks.

[19] When you have finished answering all the questions, check through your work, especially the marked questions/answers mentioned in [15] above.

4 FURTHER TIPS ON EXCELLING IN IQ AND APTITUDE TESTS

PART I: MENTAL OUTLOOK IS VERY IMPORTANT

Essay-writing at the SAT, GRE or GMAT level is distinctly different from that at the high school level. Whereas the essay writer in the high school level English Language exam is normally asked to write essays of a "descriptive" nature on a topic of interest (e.g., a visit to the zoo, the person I admire most, et al.), the essay-writing for SAT, GRE or GMAT is expected to be at a much higher intellectual plane. While at the high school level, being able to write good, clear English is more or less sufficient for doing well in the English Language paper, this is definitely not sufficient for doing well in the SAT, GRE or GMAT.

Adopt The Right Attitude

The very first step the SAT, GRE or GMAT test-taker now has to take is to change his mental attitude or mental outlook greatly. He should attempt to cultivate a **CURIOUS, CRITICAL** mind. Instead of just blindly assimilating and regurgitating information as he normally has been so accustomed to at the high school level, he should now look at information critically, i.e., study them closely with a judgmental eye, or, consider them deeply with an alert, sharp mind. In short, SAT, GRE or GMAT test-takers, in order to do well in their essay-writing, should adopt the **CORRECT ATTITUDE**. The correct attitude is to be curious, enquiring and hungry for facts.

Standards Expected

The standards expected for passing this "English Language" exam at the SAT, GRE or GMAT level are apparently pretty high.

First of all, test-takers in their essays are expected to display "maturity of thought". That is, he should be able to judge right from wrong and be able to reason things out for himself. The author would say that from the quality of the thoughts expressed in the test-taker's essay, an examiner could with a fair degree of accuracy judge the test-taker's intelligence or reasoning power.

Secondly, just as important, test-takers are expected to express their ideas clearly and well. The correct choice of words, grammar and tenses is also indicative of an intelligent, logical mind.

In other words, to do well in essay-writing, the test-taker should have a clear and logical mind. He should have some depth of thought. He should be able to play with ideas and words and be aware of their implications. He should be subtle enough to realize the various shades of ideas and meanings. This kind of mental qualities could be and has to be cultivated by the test-taker. One way of developing this mental attitude is through wide reading and engaging in arguments or debates with classmates or friends. Stimulating books, articles and essays, and even friends, are of paramount importance.

Some of these items may be unconventional, controversial and, perhaps, very stimulating. Hopefully, the reader is stimulated by the items to do research on and carry on reading further on the various subjects brought up. The author lends himself as an example for having been a very voracious reader, a "Jack of many trades". A person who has become an intellectual should excel in the essay. So, **strive to be an intellectual**.

PART II: EXCELLING IN ESSAY-WRITING

Problems Normally Faced By Test-Takers

SAT, GRE or GMAT test-takers, freshly graduated from school, probably need some time to adjust their "mental gears" to a higher level of thought.

Another not uncommon failing of SAT, GRE or GMAT test-takers is not having enough interest or time to delve into affairs of the world at large, be it science, politics, education and the like, what with the great loads of homework they might be burdened with. Time for reading the newspapers and watching the news on TV might be limited; there is perhaps also hardly time to read magazines, journals and good books.

Another weakness, which is quite common, is a weak command of the English language. This especially applies to those who did not fare well in the high school English Language exam. For this group, their foundation of the language is weak. Perhaps, they have not been properly taught the basics at school. Perhaps, they speak too much dialects at home and have insufficient exposure to the English language. They should immerse themselves more in the usage of the English language, whether in conversation or in writing. They might be spending more time reading books in some other language, e.g., French, than books written in English. The reverse should be the case.

For SAT, GRE or GMAT test-takers encountering the above-mentioned difficulties, there is no other way out but to read more English books, magazines or newspapers, speak more English at home and with friends, and, take remedial classes or tuition to shore up their weak foundation, especially so if they have not even grasped the ABCs of English grammar such as the nouns, the verbs and the tenses. (If they could not pass junior school English, neither could they be expected to pass high school English nor SAT, GRE or GMAT English.)

Tips On Writing Reasonably Good English, If You Are Weak In English

For those whose command of the English language is weak, they should observe the following simple rules:-

[1] Read as much as possible, the more the better.

[2] In your readings, observe the **writing styles** adopted by the authors or the writers.

[3] For a start, try to adopt the writing style of your favorite author (at least, till you have a reasonable good grasp of the language). For instance, the author has been "crazy" about the James Bond novels in his younger days. He has had imitated James Bond author Ian Fleming's writing style. The author remembers that Fleming liked to use swear words such as "Bastard!" in his novels. The author had, e.g., used "Bastard!" to interject in his high school essays, for which he has had generally scored high marks.

[4] If you are confident enough about your English language skills, you could develop your own personal style. To achieve this requires patience, hard work and determination.

[5] Improve your vocabulary. Get a note-book. Jot down words whose meanings you do not know, use the dictionary. Jot down the meanings of these words. Read them over and over again, from time to time (revise). Try to use these newly learnt words in your essays, writings or conversations. Application would improve your understanding of these words and ensure you do not forget them.

[6] Revise your homework, your written essays, from time to time. Note your tutor's comments if any and the errors. Tell yourself to write as instructed by your tutor and avoid making the same errors in your future essays, especially your test essay. (The author notes that some students kept repeating the same errors in their essays. It

is apparent that they had not bothered to improve, by revising their past work, for example).

[7] Remember that "practice makes perfect". Besides reading widely, you should write, write and write.

General Rules For Writing The SAT, GRE Or GMAT Essay

[1]   This is of utmost importance. In the SAT, GRE or GMAT essay test, read the instructions carefully, at least twice. Underline the **keywords** in the question you are attempting. For instance, in the question, "Religions never do anyone any good. Discuss.", you could underline the words "Religions" and "Discuss", these being the keywords. The underlining of these keywords helps to ensure that you know what you are supposed to write on (the keywords act as "reminders"), preventing you from straying into irrelevant points.

[2]   Try to keep your sentences short and simple. (Try not to make things complicated and avoid confusing yourself.)

[3]   Your sentences should each have a subject (a noun) and a predicate (a verb or action) at least.

[4]   Be logical about tenses. What has had happened (and would never happen again) should be mentioned in the past tense or past participle. What would generally take place from time to time (and still does happen) should be mentioned in the present tense.

[5]   Do not neglect commas, semi-colons, full-stops, et al. Placing these punctuation marks in the right places would make your meanings or message clear. (Misinterpretations would not occur. The meanings or message are clear. And, there is no need for the reader to guess the meanings or message.)

[6]   Attempt an essay on a subject you have a deep interest in or a great passion for. Strength of feelings or passion does make your arguments or your opinions look more impressive, as though they have been well thought out. Besides, it is much more fun to write about something

you are deeply interested in.

[7] Plan your essay carefully before writing. List down the ideas you wish to write on. Always refer back to the question to ensure you are not straying out of the point (especially to the underlined keywords as mentioned in [1]).

[8] Your essay should have a title (including the number of the question you are attempting), an introduction and an ending or conclusion. Each paragraph should focus on a main idea or theme and should lead logically from idea to idea, paragraph to paragraph.

[9] You should think carefully before writing, always referring to the keywords in the question that you have underlined, so that you do not write out of point.

[10] Always try to reflect that you have a matured, logical mind as you write. You should write and express yourself clearly to indicate that you have a clear mind.

[11] When writing, try to be as objective as possible - be coldly logical and precise. When discussing any viewpoint, consider it from all possible angles (do not look at it from just one or a few narrow angles, do not show your prejudice or prejudices).

[12] Avoid display of emotions - be emotionally detached.

[13] Remember that the examiner is more interested in your mind than your heart.

[14] You reflect your objective, logical mind by using terms such as "probably", "perhaps", "it seems", "relatively" and "it appears that" to "qualify" your statements. There are many concepts that could be classified as "grey areas", especially if they are merely your opinions, which could be both right and wrong, depending on how you look at them. Do not be dogmatic - do not reflect an inflexible mind, a mind with a fixed set of ideas, regardless of the soundness or reasonableness of the ideas.

[15] Attempt an essay topic that suits your temperament. For example, some test-takers are artistically inclined and

ideas would flow freely from their mind when they are discussing the arts. Yet some others with an argumentative outlook favor and thrive on the controversial kind of topics such as, e.g., sexual equality and religion.

[16] You should have good time-keeping and planning; write and check your essay all within the allocated time.

[17] You should make a habit of checking your facts, grammar, tenses, spellings and expressions as you write.

[18] After completing the essay, you should check it, making corrections or amendments neatly where necessary.

[19] You should also remember to write legibly and neatly. (It is pointless to write excellently if the examiner could not decipher your handwriting.)

PART III: EXCELLING IN THE COMPREHENSION TEST

The comprehension test is perhaps more difficult than the essay-writing test and may not just be a test of the test-taker's command of the English language but a test of his intelligence, or, his ability to think well and clearly, as well. Nevertheless, the comprehension test should be tackled in a systematic manner so that great success may be achieved. The following is a listing of the steps which should be taken by the test-taker sitting for the comprehension test:-

[1] Firstly, read through the passage quickly to get the gist of what it is all about.

[2] Then, run through all the test questions to get an idea of what materials from the passage are required.

[3] Reread the passage, slowly this time, trying to understand the passage more in-depth.

[4] Underline the keywords or points in the passage, or, jot down the points on a piece of rough paper.

[5] After rereading the passage, go back to the questions.

[6] If there is a choice of questions, choose those you are

most comfortable with.

[7] When attempting to answer the questions, make sure you understand or know what the questions require.

[8] Underline the keywords in the questions and make very sure you know what is required so as not to answer out-of-point. For example, when you are asked to "discuss" (give the pros and cons), do not "describe", which will render your answer irrelevant or out-of- point and, therefore, wrong.

[9] When answering the questions refer back frequently to the passage and note, underline or jot down the required points.

[10] Keep looking at the underlined keywords of the question you are attempting, to make very sure you are answering the question to the point.

[11] Make sure that your answers have all the relevant points, are logical and are grammatically correct.

[12] Check your answers sufficiently and aim for perfection. Polish them up or correct them where necessary.

[13] However, keep to the time limit and avoid spending too much time on each of the questions.

[14] For the section on explaining or giving the meanings of words or phrases in the context of the passage, you may substitute these words or phrases with words or phrases which will make sense in the context of the passage. If you have really understood the passage, substituting the words or phrases from the passage with appropriate words or phrases should not present much of a problem. If you really have problems with finding the right substitutes, you can always make an intelligent, well-considered guess.

[15] Check by replacing the words or phrases in the passage with the substitute words or phrases. Read the sentence or sentences which now contain these substitute words or phrases and ensure that the sentence or sentences are grammatically correct and make sense, modifying, making corrections to or changing the substitute words

or phrases where necessary.

PART IV: FURTHER TIPS ON WRITING GOOD ENGLISH

[1] Ideas should be to the point and logical.

[2] Ideas should be clearly expressed - do not create doubts.

[3] Language should be simple - easy to understand.

[4] Language should be grammatically correct.

[5] Writing should be convincing and interesting - show some passion or strong feeling, display maturity of thought or sophistication of mind.

PART V: FURTHER TIPS ON COMPREHENSION

[1] Read the instructions carefully and fully understand what is required.

[2] Read the passage quickly first to get a general idea.

[3] Next, run through the comprehension questions quickly to get a general idea of what is required.

[4] Read the passage again and try to understand more in-depth with the comprehension questions in mind. Underline or highlight the important points, or, make notes on rough paper.

[5] Read carefully and attempt the comprehension questions. Underline the keywords in the questions so that you would not forget or overlook what is really required and would not give irrelevant points in your answers.

[6] Ensure you fully understand the following terms which may be used in the comprehension questions:-

(i) Describe - narrate or show

(ii) Explain - give the reasons, make clear

(iii) Discuss - give the pros and cons, advantages and disadvantages

(iv) Comment - give your opinions, similar to "discuss"

(v) Compare - give the similarities and differences

between two objects/persons

(vi) List - enumerate, e.g., list item number one, item number two, item number three, and so on in consecutive order

(vii) Show - similar to "describe"

(viii) Why ....? - give the reasons, similar to "explain"

(ix) How ....? - show, similar to "describe"

(x) Define - state or give the meaning of

(xi) Give the meaning of - state the meaning of or define

(xii) Explain the meaning of - state or give the meaning of, plus providing one or more examples in order to make clear (provide more details)

[7] Answer all questions in full, complete sentences, for example:

"in a daze" means "in a state of confusion". (Answer to: Give the meaning of "in a daze".)

Do not just answer:

in a state of confusion

(which is a phrase and not a sentence, resulting in loss of marks)

[8] Check your answers and ensure they are grammatically correct, logical and relevant.

PART VI: GENERAL KNOWLEDGE, VOCABULARY, INTELLIGENCE, EXCELLING IN INTELLECTUAL WORK AND TESTS

The SAT, GRE or GMAT may be viewed as a test of general intelligence, or, an IQ test. It is practically a test of the test-taker's power of logical thinking and his power of comprehension. It may also be construed as a test of the test-taker's depth and breadth of mind, mental qualities which an IQ test may not examine effectively. The SAT, GRE or GMAT essay encompasses a wide range of subjects and topics, science, religion, politics, world affairs, economics, literature, sports, psychology, the media and communications, transportation, et al. The comprehension passage may also touch on any of these subjects and topics. The safest bet for excelling in the SAT, GRE or GMAT is to really take an active interest in all manners of intellectual matters and read as widely as possible. To excel in IQ or other aptitude tests also requires one to read widely on these tests, deconstructing them, trying them out, and so on. The famous, brilliant futurologist, Herman Kahn, had obtained the highest score ever achieved for his army IQ test by the expediency of deconstructing and cramming lots of IQ tests. Brilliance is apparently achievable through effort and hard work. (Kahn took only 20 minutes to complete the 45-minute AGCT (Army General Classification Test) and had obtained a score of 161 out of a possible maximum score of 162.)

SAT, GRE or GMAT test-takers may not realize the part wide reading plays in improving their power of comprehension, and, hence, improving their effective intelligence or IQ. Wide reading, besides helping them to excel in the SAT, GRE or GMAT, would really make them more intelligent or smarter. Not only that, it would also help them to excel in their other subjects, e.g., science and literature. An ignorant mind could never really be sharp, but be dull and narrow in outlook. According to Francis Bacon, the noted British philosopher, reading nourishes the mind. The more we know and understand the world around us, the better we are at understanding and solving any of the world's problems. We need to realize that how much of a topic we would comprehend or understand does depend on our knowledge or understanding of some topics related to it. For instance, if we are already familiar with Einstein's theory of relativity, understanding such esoteric scientific topics as quantum mechanics or superstrings would be easier for they are all somehow related, and, in mathematics, understanding the more advanced topics would require an understanding of the related, more basic topics.

Wide reading would give us insights into many different things, and, could even present to us a glimpse of the interconnectedness of the various branches of knowledge, making us effectively more intelligent, smarter or wiser. All this reading should of course be the intellectually challenging kind of reading and not just the reading of frivolous literature. The SAT, GRE or GMAT test-taker with good general knowledge is likely to be brimming with ideas where intellectual discussion and essay-writing on intellectual matters (in the SAT, GRE or GMAT) are concerned. Importantly, he is also in a better position to tackle the comprehension section of the SAT, GRE or GMAT, as his sound knowledge foundation (general knowledge) would be likely to enable him to see the links between what he already knows and the topic brought up in the comprehension passage, thus enabling him to readily understand the comprehension passage. This same phenomenon is likely to apply to his other examination subjects.

Thus, the well-read SAT, GRE or GMAT test-taker should not only be doing well in the SAT, GRE or GMAT, but in his other subjects as well. Very importantly, his great general knowledge, his great breadth of mind, should make him an effectively smarter, more intelligent, wiser person. Therefore, read, read and read intellectually challenging books and articles on science, mathematics, economics and other important topics.

Last but not least, we must not forget about having a good vocabulary, as words, including symbols, e.g., scientific and mathematical symbols, are the tools for thought. From the soft sciences to the hard sciences, and, in our everyday affairs, words are essential to effective thinking. A powerful vocabulary hence implies a powerful mind. The following quote is attributed to Marilyn vos Savant, whose IQ of 230 was the highest IQ ever measured on the Stanford-Binet intelligence test (the average IQ being 100):-

A well-developed vocabulary is the outward sign of a well-developed mind. Words are the working tools of your brain, just as surely as your hands or your eyes.

For everyone who is at all concerned about improving his mental capacity or having a sharper mind, regardless of his station in life, the information in this book should be of much help.

5 THE MOST IMPORTANT FACTOR CONTRIBUTING TO GREATER BRAIN-POWER AND INTELLIGENCE

Man prides himself on his power of reasoning, his intelligence, which gives him the upper hand over the other forms of life. Of course he realizes that even this great power of reasoning or intelligence is not perfect and has much room for improvement. We all know how difficult it is to grasp a complex reasoning in advanced mathematics or physics full of abstruse, incomprehensible symbolism. The following quote taken from the author's book on logic, *Logic: Its Proper Use [How To Think Logically]*, describes it succinctly:-

What actually is logic? We have a brain. We think. As long as we think, there should be logic. To see logic is to be aware of the implication or implications of a truth or some truths, or, a fact or some facts (or, even an untruth or some untruths, or, a lie or some lies), to be aware of the link or links of the truth(s) or fact(s) with another truth or other truths. For example, truth A implies truth B; truths A and B imply truth C, or (perhaps), truths C and D; truth A implies truths B, C and D (or more), or, truth A implies truth B, truth B implies truth C, truth C implies truth D, and the implication (or link) may continue further from truth D, et al. The truth(s) or fact(s) might be presented in any form, e.g., in the English language, even in the sign language, or, in the mathematical language or other forms of symbolism, and so might the logical deductions or implications. Logic is thus implication, implication, and more implications. From a single truth or fact, we might arrive at more truths or facts (i.e., implications). That is how human

knowledge grows. Also, from a number of truths or facts, or, propositions or statements (which might not be truths but downright falsehoods) implications (which might themselves be falsehoods if they were the results of falsehoods) might be realized. Every person should understand what the statements produced by other people, and, the "statements" produced by nature as well, imply. Logic is really implication. It would be great if our minds were more often than not alert to all such implications. This would indeed be a mind steeped in logic. But, there is a serious problem, viz., what is considered as an implication (or link) by one person might not be considered so by another person. This is the greatest problem of logic. How should this problem be dealt with? This book attempts to settle this problem. Reasoning could either proceed from causes to effects (or results), or, vice versa, i.e., proceed from effects to causes. The longer the chain of reasoning is, the more the premises there are and/or the more complex the premises are, the more difficult the reasoning would be; in such instances the reasoner has to hold many points or data in his mind at the same time while performing the act of reasoning; therefore, <u>a good memory goes hand-in-hand with good reasoning power</u>. However, one should only discuss logic with a person who is really capable of logical reasoning. But the problem is that it is difficult to judge whether a person is really capable of logical reasoning. This problem is compounded by the possibility that the person really incapable of logical reasoning regarding his very own "logic" as the correct or valid one while dismissing the true logician's logic as "nonsense". This means that logic serves no useful purpose at all if it fails to persuade or influence another person. Logic should thus not be used or applied blindly but with discretion. Logic is only justified by the end or the result. Disputes and conflicts are manifestations of the failure or weakness of logic. Winning an argument or dispute and making the other party feel that he is wrong or foolish may be an achievement for a person well-versed in logic, but if the out-argued or outwitted person takes it badly or feels hurt as a result he may hold a grudge against his victor and may even seek revenge. To avoid such an undesirable consequence everyone should use or apply logic wisely if at all so that there would be mutual respect and harmony; logic should never be used to make another person look like a fool but should only be used to make the other party accept it willingly and happily - if this happens logic would have played its rightful role, viz., bring about better changes and more happiness. Unfortunately, many egoistic people use logic to brow-beat others to make themselves feel good while the latter feel bad, resulting in unhappiness and disharmony. Logic could simply be summed up as follows - it is reason, and, there are many reasons governing human conduct; and reasons explain things and give understanding. One interesting poser: What is logic for really? Would logic be of great importance if there were only one lone surviving logical human being in the whole world after the rest of the human race had perished?

The Author's View Of Logic

Below is a proof or mathematical reasoning with unfamiliar symbolism and mathematical jargon taken from a monograph:-

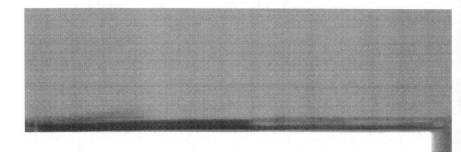

Theorem 7. 3. Let D be a domain, $S_i (i=1,2)$ two locally uniformly disjoint sets of holomorphic functions in D and p a positive integer. Let $\mathscr{F}$ be the family of the functions $f(z)$ satisfying the following conditions:

1^0 $f(z)$ is holomorphic in D.

2^0 There are two functions $\varphi_i(z) \in S_i (i=1,2)$ such that each of the two functions $f(z) - \varphi_i(z)$ $(i=1,2)$ has at most p distinct zeros in D.

Then the family $\mathscr{F}$ is quasi-nrmal in D of order p at most.

Proof. Consider a suquence of functions $f_n(z)$ $(n=1,2,\cdots)$ of the family $\mathscr{F}$. Then to each $f_n(z)$ correspond $\varphi_{ni}(z) \in S_i(i=1,2)$ such that each of $f_n(z) - \varphi_{ni}(z)$ $(i=1,2)$ has at most p distinct zeros in D. Accordingly the function

$$g_n(z) = \frac{f_n(z) - \varphi_{n1}(z)}{\varphi_{n2} - \varphi_{n1}(z)}$$

has at most p distinct zeros in D and the same is true for $g_n(z) - 1$. By Corollary 5. 11, the family $\{g_n(z)\ (n=1,2,\cdots)\}$ is quasi-normal in D of order p at most. Hence from the sequence $g_n(z)$ $(n=1,2,\cdots)$ we can extract a subsequence $g_{n_k}(z)$ $(k=1,2,\cdots)$ converging locally uniformly to a holomorphic function or to ∞ in a domain $D - \sigma$, where σ is a set consisting of at most p points of D. Making use of the condition that $S_i (i=1,2)$ are locally uniformly disjoint, we see as in the proof of Theorem 7. 1, that either the sequence $f_{n_k}(z)$ $(k=1,2,\cdots)$ converges locally uniformly to ∞ in $D - \sigma$ or we can extract from the sequence $f_{n_k}(z)$ $(k=1, 2,\cdots)$ a subsequence $f_{m_s}(z)$ $(s=1,2,\cdots)$ converging locally uniformly to a holomorphic function in $D - \sigma$. This proves Theorem 7. 3.

In the above proof (mathematical reasoning) of Theorem 7. 3, we have to understand what the unfamiliar symbolism represent and to be able to retain them in memory for at least a short while (short-term memory) in order to follow the proof. We also need to refer back to Corollary 5. 11, which was presented earlier, and to be able to hold it in memory for at least a short while too (short-term memory again), while trying to follow the proof or reasoning. Isn't it now obvious that memory has an important part to play in grasping the proof of Theorem 7. 3? If the above theorem and proof were presented in plain, simple English instead of unfamiliar symbolism and mathematical jargon, they could have been perfectly understood by anyone including the lay person. This incomprehensibility is not unlike the incomprehensibility of a legal document full of legal jargon. It is evident that the professional mathematician and lawyer take pride in the incomprehensibility of their work to the uninitiated and the lay person and hence uphold their "professionalism".

Let's touch a little more on mathematical reasoning. A distinctive feature of the above proof or mathematical reasoning is the unfamiliar symbolism and its apparent ambiguity, which is unlike our familiar English alphabet and numerals. Recapitulating here, to grasp the above proof one needs to find out what the symbols in the proof represent. After that one needs to keep in mind or remember the symbols and what they represent as one follows the reasoning. This is bound to be a problem. If one's memory, in this case short-term memory, is untrained and poor one will have problems remembering these unfamiliar symbols and their meanings, as well as following the reasoning. Some mathematical reasoning may not be that straightforward. The whole structure of the proof or reasoning may be based on some earlier lemmas, corollaries or axioms (which the proof or reasoning may refer to). Remembering the latter and really understanding them with their difficult symbolism is another hurdle to clear, which will depend again on the efficacy of one's memory. Hence, the importance of a well-trained, efficient memory.

We are not unfamiliar with the rote learning or memory work of our student days. Though exams may profess to test a student's analytical ability or intelligence, the student will not be able to analyze a subject if he cannot remember some facts relating to that subject - the student needs to reason with facts which he has to be able to recall from memory (unless it is an open-book exam, which is not common).

Therefore, the most important factor contributing to superior brain-power is a good memory. To reason well, we need to be able to hold facts, steps or ideas in the short-term memory at least while the reasoning is in progress. If our short-term memory were not able to retain these facts or steps, then the reasoning process would be stalled. We would then have to retrace our steps, e.g., by figuring out or looking for the facts before continuing. Time would then be lost and effort would have been wasted. This applies especially in the case involving complicated mathematical reasoning utilizing many lines of symbols and theorems which have to be borne in mind or memory in order to comprehend the reasoning. Even in sitting the IQ or aptitude tests, short-term memory is important, for the same reason explained above.

How to have a good short-term memory? First of all, cultivating a focused or forced concentration at the task at hand is necessary. All this can be achieved through training or practice. The author recommends the following mind training. Attempt to memorize a list of letters, numbers or words, increasing the length of the list with time and improvement. For example, start with ten random numbers (or, letters, or, words, or, a combination of them), as follows, increasing the quantity of random numbers with time:-

3, 9, 8, 7, 6, 4, 3, 2, 4, 9

To keep these numbers fixed in your short-term memory, focus on each of these numbers for say several seconds or whatever suitable time-span. After doing this for all the ten random numbers and memorizing them (by repeating them to yourself over and over again until you have committed them to memory), write down the list of these ten random numbers in the order in which they appear in the list from memory. After all this, compare the lists and check for correctness. With time and improvement you should be able to memorize 20, 30, 40, 50 or more random numbers.

With considerable practice your short-term memory should improve and you would be able to think and reason better; the short-term memory should be developed to such an extent that long sequences of facts could be naturally, automatically and quite effortlessly recalled when needed.

However, the reader may choose or implement other similar forms of mental training to improve his short-term memory capability. With an improved short-term memory capability, the reader's effective brain-power, mental capacity or intelligence would also be improved. Brain-power is actually about the brain being able to operate efficiently. With an improved short-term memory capability, this brain efficiency would of course be improved. The mathematical genius John von Neumann, e.g., had a photographic memory, and was capable of memorizing book chapters and phone directories verbatim, performing complex mental calculations and comprehending abstruse reasoning at lightning speed. His genius had been acknowledged by all his peers, who frequently consulted him on unsolved problems, and he was possibly the most intelligent person in the world.

It is really important that the reader improves his or her

short-term memory capability by suitable mental training, any sort of mental training as long as it would improve his or her short-term memory capability. Finally, the reader should practice applying his short-term memory capability, e.g., by reading and trying to understand texts with convoluted reasoning involved, such as mathematical and technical books.

6 HOW GENIUSES DEVELOP THEIR MENTAL CAPACITY

It is a moot question whether brilliance is inborn or nurtured. Brilliance however appears to be a combination of both of these. Researchers have come up with the 10,000-hour rule, i.e., it has been found that accomplishments of genius are generally the result of about 10,000 hours of consistent hard work and practice. This means that to be a genius one needs to work consistently hard, for 10,000 hours at least. Mozart had spent most of his waking hours on music. The great basketball player Michael Jordan had trained extremely hard to be at the top of his game. Einstein had to devote about ten years to developing his theories of relativity. Newton the scientific genius had also overworked himself to the point of breakdown. It seems that geniuses are highly motivated, hard-working and obsessive high achievers. Nurture or training seems to play a big part in the development of genius or high ability.

Some geniuses had been trained and home-schooled by their parents to be geniuses. For example, John Stuart Mill the famous British philosopher (who had been home-schooled), William Sidis the boy genius, and Norbert Weiner another boy genius, had been trained and brought up by their parents for great intellectual achievements; because of the great pressure placed on them to achieve John Stuart Mill and William Sidis had in fact suffered mental breakdowns.

The training of the mental faculties for self-improvement is something which is possible, in fact feasible. For example, intellectually challenged youngsters have been trained and have their mental capacity improved to the point where they are able to take care of themselves, even attending a normal school and coping there.

The average IQ of people now is higher than the average IQ of their predecessors, the average IQ increasing every year or so, an effect which is known as the Flynn effect. Does this imply that people now are really inherently or naturally more intelligent than their forefathers? It has been surmised that this is not really the case. The standard of living now is much higher than in the past. People now are living in a better environment, with better diet, better health facilities, better educational opportunities, in short better nurture. The average height of people now, e.g., has also increased; people are now taller, bigger, healthier and apparently more intelligent (e.g., scoring more A's in their exams) due likely to a better environment.

It is said that a stimulating environment improves intelligence. Reading is also said to be good for improving the capability of the brain. But the most potent way of improving one's intelligence appears to be highly motivated self-directed mental training. Consider the training for the mathematical tripos, competitive mathematics exams conducted in Cambridge University in the past but are now abolished. Achieving the number one rank of senior wrangler in the mathematical tripos was no mean feat. Typically these mathematical scholars had to be under the tutelage of mathematicians many of whom had themselves been senior wranglers in the Cambridge mathematical tripos who were familiar with the ins and outs and tricks of the mathematical tripos. Senior wranglers were generally top mathematical scholars who had been so well-trained by their tutors that they could tackle the tough mathematical problems of the tripos practically instinctively without second thoughts or batting an eyelid and with great speed. Like the IQ test, candidates were not expected to be able to answer all the questions in the exam, with speed being a premium. In this respect, well-trained senior wranglers could be compared to well-trained race-horses. The mathematical tripos was actually in effect a very difficult and advanced IQ test. To excel in IQ and aptitude tests, the reader should follow the example of these senior wranglers, i.e., train himself to be so familiar with the test material that he could tackle them practically effortlessly and with speed, as the famous futurist Herman Kahn mentioned in Chapter 4 had done.

Doing well in IQ and aptitude tests may open doors for us and may provide us a great sense of achievement and confidence in our ability. But this will not make us a true genius per se. It is what we actually do with our evident high intelligence, what we actually achieve, i.e., how creative we really are, that counts, that makes others really respect us as a genius. In short, it is really our contributions to society which count, the high IQ only indicating that we are capable of making contributions to society. However, creativity has been regarded as an entity quite distinct from high IQ. It is thought that it is not necessary to have an astronomical IQ to be highly creative, a merely superior IQ will do for high creativity. For high creativity, the person should learn how to make use of his unconscious mind for creative ideas. The unconscious mind works mysteriously and produces creative ideas in a leisurely, unrushed manner as compared to the conscious, intelligent mind; e.g., creative ideas or flashes of genius may suddenly appear out of nowhere, for instance when one is on the plane, on the train, on the beach, in the shopping mall, in the bathroom, or resting, when one least expects them. Therefore, it may pay to actually give more attention to our creative, unconscious mind than our conscious, intelligent mind; high IQ may actually not matter as much as high creativity. All this apparent obsession with high IQ in our society may be unnecessary. On the other hand, creativity is also another attribute of the mind, one of the so-called multiple intelligences of the mind, and should be regarded as an aspect of intelligence (or IQ).

Lewis Terman had in fact conducted a study of gifted youngsters in his attempt to prove that those gifted with high intelligence would generally be successful in life. He had subjected a group of youngsters to IQ tests. He then tracked the progress of those who had scored high on the tests, these high scorers having a whopping average IQ of 151, for the next 35 years. It was found that though this high scoring group (who had been called Termites) had generally done well in life none of them had won Nobel prizes or other similar accolades, a possible achievement expected of them because of their high intelligence. On the other hand, two of the youngsters who had taken the same IQ tests but did not make the cut, William Shockley and Louis Alvarez, had gone on to win Nobel prizes for their scientific achievements. All this shows that high IQ alone is not sufficient for high achievement. Hard work, motivation, persistence and other personal characteristics, and even opportunity and luck, are just as important, if not more important.

Intelligence is also evidently related to intuition. A person may be intelligent and capable of reasoning and comprehension. However, it is his intuition or hunch which will guide his thinking, the direction of his thinking. Some geniuses are highly creative because of their great intuition, e.g., the mathematical geniuses Bernard Riemann, Henri Poincare and Srinivasa Ramanujan had many great theorems conceived by their intuition before they themselves could confirm the correctness of the theorems with proofs, while many other mathematical geniuses created new theorems based on solid reasoning rather than intuition. A highly intelligent person might just instantly grasp the correctness of an abstruse mathematical reasoning due to his great intuition. Highly intuitive people might be capable of mind-reading and predicting the future. There had been cases of such intuitive people whose mental feats had amazed. All humans are however more or less intuitive. Intuition is one of the mysterious qualities of the mind which deserves greater study. Everyone should try to develop his intuitive powers.

7 HOW TO BE EVEN SMARTER

Though high intelligence as is evidenced by excellence in IQ or aptitude tests or excellence in academic pursuits is important, a person thus endowed may not really be that smart after all. In fact IQ and aptitude tests, and, educational tests and assessments evaluate a narrow spectrum of abilities or intelligences, more on the linguistic and logical-mathematical intelligences. The various intelligences (multiple intelligences) have been brought up in Chapter 2, but that chapter only touches on eight types of intelligence. The human brain is extremely complex and it definitely has many other types of intelligence which the person may not realize that he possesses.

A person may be highly intelligent but he may not be wise, and, he may also not be objective. He may also lack emotional intelligence which is now considered by many to be more important than high IQ for success in life. Can these qualities be easily acquired? It is hard to answer this question. Many highly intelligent people are somehow foolish in certain ways, which seems contradictory here. Many highly intelligent people are also immoral or even downright evil. On this last point about immorality and evilness, to be moral or to understand the principles of morality or ethics a person needs to be sufficiently intelligent. Do not expect a mentally challenged or insane person to be able to tell right from wrong, to be able to understand moral principles; a person of low intelligence may not know the implications or repercussions of his actions which may cause harm without him being aware of it. On the other hand, a wise person knows the moral principles and makes it an important point to act according to these principles, having a broad view of the world. He may, e.g., be versed in Confucian principles and concerned about the truth, i.e., he likes to know the truths about life and nature.

Being wise, the person is also objective, i.e., wisdom and objectivity go hand in hand and are compatible with one another. Wisdom comes with experience, learning and wide reading which will all lead to the truths.

No matter how high a person's IQ is, if he is not objective he will not be truly intelligent for being objective means being able to face reality and accept reality no matter how unpalatable that reality is, i.e., he will not deceive himself by inventing some excuses to make the unpalatable reality palatable, e.g., he may excuse or justify his low score on an IQ test by an invalid reason such as the biased nature of the IQ test, he is too intelligent for his IQ to be measurable by a mere IQ or aptitude test, et al. The wise and objective person may just face reality and accept his low IQ score and may do more practice IQ tests to improve on his score, which is actually an intelligent response or behavior.

If a person is not objective, i.e., biased, though he may be very intelligent, e.g., he may even excel in an IQ test, he will be wrong, even idiotic, where the bias is concerned, and if his action is based on this bias he may cause harm to himself and others. To be rid of the bias and to accept the reality no matter how unpalatable it is he will be entirely right or correct and will thereby avoid causing harm to himself and others. To be biased is actually to be wrong for a bias is an untruth or falsehood. How can a biased person be truly or totally intelligent? At most he is only partially intelligent, i.e., intelligent only on the unbiased aspects of his thoughts. Therefore, an objective, wise person who is only concerned with having the truth no matter how unpalatable the truth is is a truly intelligent person. He does not kid himself or live in denial of the facts or truth.

Hence, a person can be even smarter by being objective, by having the courage to face and accept the truth no matter how unpalatable the truth is, for he will be correct, while the biased person lives in denial of the facts or truth, i.e., fools himself, buries himself in falsehood, in effect becoming a fool who victimizes himself by embracing a falsehood - he is fooled by himself. A biased person who embraces falsehood and lives a lie is like an insane person who lives in a make-believe world. Unfortunately the biased person in his eagerness to soothe his sensitive ego by being biased may not be aware of this foolishness of his; in this state he will stay a fool.

To be objective is actually to be self-aware, to be able to look at oneself as an objective outsider would look at oneself, to be detached from one's ego and feelings, to be only concerned with the truth. This is actually real, cold intelligence. How many living in this world are truly objective in their outlook? There do not appear to be many.

Being objective is more important than having high mental capacity. A person with high mental capacity but lacks objectivity, i.e., he is biased or prejudiced, is in effect a fool where his bias or prejudice is concerned. Hence, do not be a fool, be smart, be objective. Don't we always respect an objective person and despise a biased, prejudiced person?

It is important to improve our OQ (objectivity quotient) besides improving our IQ. Both OQ and IQ should accompany one another hand-in-hand. In fact, they are both linked. Objectivity can be regarded as one of the multiple intelligences of the human brain.

Finally, to be really smart means to be accepted as smart by one's peers, to be able to have good influence on one's peers with one's smartness. There is no useful purpose in being smart by being ignored by one's peers or worse, being regarded as a fool by them. It is important to have a high illumination quotient (IQ) besides a high intelligence quotient (IQ), i.e., to be able to project an image of high intelligence besides having a high intelligence. How to be accepted by one's peers? We can be accepted by one's peers by having high emotional intelligence. Emotional intelligence is the new buzzword in psychology. It is social intelligence, the ability to understand others' feelings, get along with others and win their support. Research has shown that success in life depends more on emotional intelligence than high mental capacity. At the end of the day, no matter how intelligent or capable we are, we have to work with others as a team. Thus, understanding others, being able to persuade and motivate others, and being able to have the cooperation or support of others are important for success in any field of work. It is highly important to improve our emotional intelligence, our emotional sensitivity, besides improving our brain-power. Fortunately, improving our emotional intelligence is not that difficult. We just need the will to do so, to interact more with others and to try to understand others more. There are also many books on emotional intelligence now which can be consulted.

As technology is changing at a great space, we should be willing to keep up by learning new things by reading widely and even attending courses. We should take challenges and keep improving and expanding our mind. Reading is one of the best ways of achieving this. Reading will increase our knowledge. With more knowledge we can generate new ideas, be more creative and think better.

8 EPILOGUE

The mind is a multiplicity of many intelligences but it will be difficult or impossible to be good in all the various intelligences. The kinds of intelligences one needs to develop will depend on one's area of work or interest, e.g., scientists need to have a highly developed logical-mathematical intelligence, writers a highly developed linguistic intelligence, singers a highly developed musical intelligence, sports men a highly developed bodily-kinesthetic intelligence, et al.

The more intelligences one is able to develop the more versatile and intelligent one will be. A person may be very strong, e.g., in one intelligence and not so in other intelligences - he may be regarded as talented, or, gifted in that intelligence. Most people are gifted in only a few intelligences while the versatile person gifted in many intelligences appears a rarity. However, people nowadays need to specialize, to develop their talent or skill in a field of choice, rather than being a jack of all trades. But it does no harm to develop other intelligences, to take up other interests or hobbies, besides being specialized in one intelligence or skill. Who knows? These other skills may come in handy one day.

However, besides a high IQ, we should also have a high EQ (emotional quotient), i.e., high emotional intelligence, which is described in Chapter 7. As is described in Chapter 7, EQ appears to be more important than IQ. With a high EQ we can ensure that our IQ is appreciated by others whereby it will be able to serve a useful purpose. However, many highly intelligent people lack EQ, not being able to get along with others, and being sidetracked as a result. EQ is important even for a genius, e.g., the mathematical genius John von Neumann evidently had a high EQ besides a high IQ - his principle was never to tell someone he was wrong or argue with him especially in front of others as it would only antagonize the person and not solve any problem - he was tactful, able to understand others' feelings, and got along with practically everybody, being good at entertaining others with jokes, humble, very good with children, being fond of toys, admired by all for his incredible intelligence, for being able to jump five blocks ahead of practically everyone in thought, such was his speed of thought and intelligence - not surprisingly he had been an influential consultant to government and private industry, having helped to develop the atomic bomb and the computer with his genius.

We need to develop both our IQ and EQ, especially the latter; in other words, we need to develop both mental capacity and emotional sensitivity, both of which being part of our multiple intelligences.

BIBLIOGRAPHY

1. Logic: Its Proper Use [How To Think Logically], Kerwin Mathew, *Kindle*, 2012

Made in the USA
Middletown, DE
23 November 2018